A Minute Before Lobolo

MOTHA KA MTSHALI

Copyright © Motha ka Mtshali 2020

All rights reserved.

No part of this book may be reproduced in any manner, mechanically or electronically, including tape or other audio recordings and photocopying, without the written permission of the author, except for reasonable excerpts for research and reviewing purposes.

ISBN: 978-1-77605-652-1
e-ISBN: 978-1-77605-651-4

Published by Kwarts Publishers
www.kwartspublishers.co.za

ACKNOWLEDGEMENTS

Writing a book is hard; I can't even recall the number of times I gave up on it. None of this would have been possible without my wife, Thuli. Thank you *sthandwasam* for being my moon and stars during those dark days. You never got tired of listening to me and giving me advice on very sensitive and tough issues, from the very first page to the last you've been with me *"all the way, all the way. All the waa-waa-way!"* (In Ringo Madlingozi's voice).

To Mpho Maringa, my former colleague, thank you for the support and encouragement you gave me during the early drafts.

My eternal gratitude to my first editor Sibongile Fisher, you went an extra mile on those first edits and basically gave direction and intelligibility to my voice. And to Sheena Carnie, my second editor, thank you for wrapping my thoughts up and giving my narrative a face-beat.

Lastly, thanks to my parents, Wilbert 'Mathangetshitshi' Mtshali and Zodwa Doris Motha, this book wouldn't have been possible without you; literally the author wouldn't be here today thanking you for the life you gave him.

Contents

	INTRODUCTION	9
1	FROM FATHER TO SON	13
2	WHAT KIND OF A MAN ARE YOU?	21
3	SHE'S HUMAN FIRST	27
4	BEFORE LOBOLO	33
5	WHAT MEN THINK WOMEN WANT	47
6	RELATIONSHIP / MARRIAGE	55
7	LOVE	61
8	LOVE MEETS RELATIONSHIP	65
9	TOXIC MASCULINITY	71
10	SEX	75
11	DIMINISHING SEX LIFE	79
12	INFIDELITY	83
13	WHITE ELEPHANT IN THE ROOM	89
14	TOUCHY SUBJECTS	93
15	WHAT MEN WANT	103
	CONCLUSION	107

INTRODUCTION

GROWING UP I COULDN'T IMAGINE a future that didn't feature marriage in it. Getting married was one of my dreams in life, partly because the role models I had and the successful people I admired were all married. Martin Luther King Jr., Malcolm X, Steve Biko, Myles Munroe, Nelson Mandela, Steve Jobs and even one of the richest men in the world — Bill Gates — are all married. There is something about marriage that brings order and a sense of purpose to a man's life.

I started to look at the older men around me — married men and bachelors alike — and analysed the vast difference between the two. Married men were always neat, respectable and just decent citizens; on the other hand the bachelors seemed like a shadow of the former, lonely and hardened bythe regrets of having once "played" a good woman. That is what I observed in my late teenage years and early 20s. So when, after varsity, I met the woman of my dreams who ticked all the boxes, I made the decision to get married at the age of 23.

"Is she pregnant?" I was frequently asked by friends and colleagues.

"Just knock her up if you love her that much, not this marriage nonsense," a concerned colleague advised me one day on our way to work. He couldn't understand why a young man with so much potential for being a player — what is called an F-boy in current lingo — would want to settle down and burden himself with married life. Sadly that's the kind of advice you get from most guys if you want to get married, especially at a young age. "Give her a child to trap her because marriage will trap you instead," they say.

But I was in love and turned a deaf ear to what people said, and rightly so. After all, the only prerequisite for marriage was love and God knows I have lots of that. I believed that if you could love your woman unconditionally and be faithful to her you wouldn't experience any problems in your marriage. Happy wife, happy life, right? Wrong. After months of saving for lobolo and depriving myself of the carefree life — YOLO — my peers were living, I managed to pay most of it, *umfaziakaqedwa phela,* and my woman packed all her belongings in a kist and came home with me to start a new life — from Vereeniging to Tembisa.

My honeymoon stage of love being enough was short lived. Every time we had issues my wife would pack up her belongings and go back home! It seemed that the more I begged her to stay, the more I fuelled her desire to leave. I really couldn't understand why my unconditional love didn't produce the desired results.

One day, while talking about women over a game of soccer with my brother's friend, he shared with me that his wife also left him every time they had a fight. *Mameshani!* I was all ears now in anticipation of a solution to my problems. At least I was not the only one going through this.

"So, what did you do to make it stop?" I asked, trying to mask the excitement that was building inside me.

"I stopped caring."

He didn't seem bothered by what he had just said, but I was shocked. Whenever his wife threatened to leave he'd tell her to leave and apparently that's how she stopped that behaviour. I generally don't believe in tough love, but due to my inexperience I decided to try it in my own marriage.

The next time we had a fight my wife did what she normally did — packed her bags and told me she was leaving — only this time she wasn't prepared for what was to come next. I took my car keys and walked out. At the threshold, without turning to look at her, I told her to call me as soon as she got home. Guess what? Hours later I got a text from her which read something like, "Please bring some food if you can. I haven't eaten the whole day." What? She didn't leave? It worked!

I was confused and only understood what had happened when, while doing research for this book, I came across a term known as the "Principle of least interest" which is one of the indicators of power in interpersonal relationships. It suggests that the power lies in the hands of the person who cares the least about the relationship. This term was coined in 1938 bysociologist Willard Waller, who argued that one way to gain power in a relationship was to withhold love.

It subsequently dawned on me that marriage is not only about love — there are other dynamics too, like power, in how men and women relate. To be a better husband I needed to understand these relationship dynamics. I had to learn many new things and understand the basics of how men and women function in a marriage. I embarked on a four-year journey of research, reading books about marriage and having conversations with other married men, all in an effort to understand the dynamics and challenges that come with marriage life and how men deal with them. While undertaking my research I was amazed at how little men knew about marriage and how ill-prepared we men are for marriage. This is how the idea for this book came about.

There are a lot of young men out there in a similar position to the one in which I found myself soon after I got married;

they think love and being faithful is all that one needs to have a healthy marriage. However, there are other things besides lack of love and infidelity that build resentment in a marriage, like not helping around the house, for example, and I wanted to share my experiences and what I've learned to help others avoid the pitfalls.

One of the first things I realized is that some acts of love might not necessarily make the other party happy but could, nonetheless, strengthen the marriage. Sometimes marriage means taking decisions that may be perceived as unloving by your partner, but they still benefit your marriage. However other times, because of a lack of knowledge, we use outdated advice or techniques that do more harm than good in our marriages. In many circles men are still discouraged from opening up and sharing their fears and thus we continue to breed "strong" men who are not fit for marriage. My hope for this book is that it will help the reader to have more understanding and feel more equipped to be a great husband to his wife.

1

FROM FATHER TO SON

THE ADVICE I GOT FROM my father — way before I even thought of getting married — was that for me to have a long-lasting and happy marriage I should never show my pay slip to my wife. As much as that seemed unfair (my first thought was "crazy"), I figured it must have worked for him because he was married to my mother for more than 30 years until his death in 2016. However, I'm not my father and we're not living in the 1980s.

My point here is that there is a generational gap between the newlyweds of today and the people giving us advice on marriage. Back in the day, most men used to leave their pay slips in their lockers at work to avoid showing them to their wives or having their wives accidently find them in a pocket. Well, I can't actually attest to the truth of this, but those are the stories I never got tired of listening to, told time and again with zeal by the old men in my township and at church. It might seem absurd when one observes this using today's lens, but back then it was the norm — at least to those who were doing it.

Back then it seemed there was nothing complex when it came to the roles in marriage — a man worked and provided for his family while a woman took care of the children and made the house feel homely. Simple. I remember how my dad would come home from work tired and smelling like a mixture of rusting iron, his own sweat and that of the people he was crammed with on the train. He would eat and go straight to bed. If the house was clean and there was a home-cooked meal every evening, my dad was a happy man. If her children were provided for and there was a roof over our heads, my mother was happy.

I didn't feel like my father really loved my mother in the way a woman should be loved, or rather in a love language that speaks to me. I never saw them going out on a date or walking down the street holding hands — the stuff that couples do. Even when we were walking with them as kids my father would be ahead, walking in his long strides, while we followed behind jogging in between his steps.

However, when I asked my mother if she felt loved by my father, she said yes. "But how?" I asked. I was expecting that she'd say something like he would massage her feet after we were put to bed at night or something along the lines of affection and intimacy. To my surprise, her reply was that he clothed us, fed us and came back home every night. Nothing spelt love more than that for her. Her expectations were met, and what could spell love more than that? It didn't matter how romantic you were, if you failed to provide for your children my mother wouldn't have felt like you loved her — not because there's something wrong with being romantic, but because love means nothing when one's expectations are not being met.

What my father did for my mother wouldn't be enough for many women today. Why? Because the way we perceive love and marriage changes from generation to generation — one's perception of love and marriage is very much dependent on the society one's born and reared in at the time. For example, today it's okay to help your wife with the dishes and changing the baby's diaper, but should the guy's parents hear of it they would think their son *udlisiwe* or *ufakelweikorobela*. However, part of my wife's expectation is for me to clean, cook and take care of the kids in the house — an abomination to my mother's generation.

Most of us today — the '80s kids — get marriage advice from a different generation, and when we get married we realize that our modern *makoti* is wired differently to our mothers. This emerging generation of independent women who require quality time and romance is something most men of the older generation have no experience of and it therefore becomes hard for the current generation to apply what they've learned from their parents' marriages.

I can't imagine a discussion between my father and me with me seeking advice on how to deal with household chores in my house. He would probably tell me to put my foot down and demand that my wife fulfil her duties if she still wants to be a daughter emaNtshalini. But that is not possible. Not because my wife works the same hours a day as I do, and not because she's not domesticated enough — no! Rather because her expectation of marriage is to have a husband who helps around the house. That is why it is very important to know what your woman's expectations in a marriage are right from the start. Most men make the mistake of marrying someone because she meets *their* expectations in every way, but forget that *her* expectations are just as important for the marriage to be successful. You can't marry a person who's career orientated when your dream woman is a housewife.

This book, to a certain extent, gives one a sneak peek into a modern marriage and how most men deal with it. The problem with most couples whoare not yet married is that they want to learn about marriage once they've crossed that bridge, when in actual fact they should do their research before they get married. Once you're in it there's no turning back. This book is both for fellas who are not yet married and for newlywed husbands.

For those men who have crossed the lobolo threshold this book is meant to calm their fears by telling them that they are not alone in whatever they may be experiencing in their marriage. If you still find other women attractive or experience a diminishing sex life, my man, you are not alone — it happens. What discourages most men and results in them quitting while the marriage is in its embryonic stage is the same thing that discourages most Christians who quit church: Expectations.

There is a general sense that Christianity is for sinners, but the Christian lifestyle is a narrow road that makes for a hard fall if you slip. This is why people quit, because they have to keep up appearances, they are not allowed to question and they are stripped of their agency. I believe that the perception of marriage is the same — a narrow road that makes for a hard fall if you slip. The expectations are too high, you have to keep up appearances, you fear that you will be stripped of your agency, and the idea of being tied down is daunting.

When I got married I thought certain things I used to do as a single man would simply vanish. Unfortunately — and it's the same in our churches — people are misled into thinking that marriage will make certain habits evaporate as soon as you say "I do". I thought as soon as I got married I would stop looking at other women or be immune to any sexual advances they made towards me. I seriously thought marriage would turn off that switch. But it didn't. Once I realized that, I felt like I wasn't ready for my new situation and felt unworthy to be with this wonderful woman I'd married. However, my confidence was reinstated when I came across a study in

Myles Munroe's book *Understanding the Purpose and Power of Men,* where it states that, "a man's brain has a physiological response to seeing a beautiful woman that is comparable to his response to food. Apparently when a man sees a beautiful woman the pleasure circuits in his brain react. This is a physical response, part of a male's design." I realized that I, like many others out there, beat myself up over things that are not affecting me uniquely but happen to other men as well. That's not to say that it is "right" to do so, but it's just how nature is; the only control you have over it is how you choose to respond to it.

For the ones who are yet to lobolo, take this book as a list of ingredients you see printed on the labels of food items. This list of ingredients is there to help you to make an informed decision. Sadly, most people, especially the church, are afraid of pointing out the challenges that come with relationships or marriage, and when these issues do get raised they simply gloss over them. It is every person's right and responsibility to know what they are getting themselves into.

Nothing in this life is perfect and marriage is no different, but the church and media will sell us the idea that it is. Even if you get your perfect wedding it doesn't mean you'll have a perfect marriage. They make people believe that marriage should be perfect in order for us to be happy and, should you be unhappy, even for a moment, then you're told you should question the relationship or marriage. That's not right though.

Think about it this way: We all know that raising children is expensive, but we continue having them regardless because, in the end, in between the sleepless nights and going to work in a torpid state, we know they bring us joy. It should be like that with marriage.

I believe women are better equipped for marriage than men. In a sense they get into it already knowing that it is not entirely about themselves but the other person as well;

this is because they get loads of subliminal marriage advice from a very young age and are almost groomed for marriage. For example, I would hear my mother occasionally saying to my sister that if she was lazy to cook and wash dishes she wouldn't last a day in marriage. "If you do this and that your marriage will be bliss," she'd say.

In my early days of marriage a part of me thought this whole idea of teaching a woman not about marriage, but rather how to serve and coddle a man, was silly and outdated. However, in my research for this book I realized that there's really nothing wrong with the advice itself but there's everything wrong with the weight that the advice places on women.

Here's an illustration to help you understand what I mean: Growing up in an informal settlement meant that we didn't have a tap in our yard but had to use the communal tap which was 100 or 200 metres away from our shack. Every evening my brother and I were tasked with getting water from the tap using a bucket — a recycled 20 litre cooking oil container that my mother got from her *mlungu*. For us to get home in peace and with the same excitement that we left in, we had to evenly distribute the weight of the bucket between the two of us by each holding a strap attached to either side of the bucket. Now apply this story to the way marriage is set up. The reality today is that society sends both partners to get water (marriage) but expects the woman to be the only one who carries the bucket.

Therein lies the problem; we don't see anybody training men on how to treat a woman. The weight and responsibility of marriage is placed on a woman, and although our role as men is not clear, we know for sure that we must be coddled and pampered. No, I'm wrong. Our role as men, and I'm sure everybody knows this, is to be a leader in a marriage; *inhlokoyekhaya*. One thing that most men forget, though, is that being a leader means that you have been placed in a position to serve. Leadership in marriage is about service to your wife. I was never taught that serving my wife, except in bed, was part of my responsibilities. That is where the problem lies — men are not taught how to serve women from a very young age in the same way my mother did with my sister; men are not taught that the responsibility to make marriage work lies with them as well.

I believe that men need to be taught from an early age how to treat a woman and all about marriage. I'm baffled by the tradition of giving a couple marriage counselling a week before their marriage because the whole purpose of telling people the realities of marriage is so that they can decide whether or not they'd like to get married one day. It is important for every human being who wants to get married to have knowledge about marriage before they commit themselves to the institution.

Even a simple thing such as purchasing an engagement ring required more knowledge and proved to be far more complex than I had anticipated. When I bought my wife — then my girlfriend — an engagement ring, I had to learn about different types of diamonds, how to take care of them and the certificates that come with them that guarantee the quality of the stone. I saw this task of buying a ring as trivial, however I needed to gain enough knowledge in order to make a good decision. This exercise, in retrospect, is how one should approach marriage — long before the ceremony that officially makes you man and wife. How many of us men get into marriage without having read even a single book about it? When it comes to marriage the knowledge of it is somehow down-played by the proverbial phrase *sizobona-phambili* — the biggest lie we tell ourselves to sleep better at night, to blanket our fears in ignorance and to lull our concerns with the comfort it offers.

In this book I'm not trying to paint a beautiful picture about marriage but rather a realistic one. This is not to scare or discourage anyone who wants to get married. Rather, it is to inform couples and newlyweds about the reality of married life and personally, a far more superior form of relationship you wouldn't want to miss out on. Like Lauryn Hill said, "Fantasy is what people want, but reality is what they need."

2
WHAT KIND OF A MAN ARE YOU?

MOST MEN JUST WANT TO see themselves married without considering the kind of woman they want. We think that women are all the same — that what they want in life and the marital roles that are expected of them will all be the same. In my circle of friends, for example, we were all raised by women who, in modern terms, would be called housewives. They basically did everything in the house — they were maids in the morning, cooks in the evening and nurses at night. What we expect from a woman is largely informed by what we saw our mothers do, but we forget that not all women are like that.

Some woman are career orientated and don't want to live the rest of their lives confined within the walls of their homes. And we men are like that as well — there are men who don't feel comfortable dating career orientated women and there are those who find housewives mundane and unstimulating. What kind of a man are you my dear reader?

The answer to this question will help you avoid conflicting visions in your marriage.

It is of paramount importance that you know if you would prefer a housewife or a career woman. A housewife is a woman we are all familiar with — a woman whose main occupation is caring for her family and creating a safe and warm environment for her family to grow in. In some extremes this woman marries to survive — perhaps she doesn't have many options in life as she lacks exposure to the working world. It must be understood, though, that more often than not it is a predestined arrangement setup by a patriarchal society and not a choice. The woman may be conscious of her situation but society has trained her to ignore all those issues she may have with that position in order to maintain peace in the house. That is how marriage has been sold to them.

For those women — women like my mother — in that position their role and importance in the family structure are often undermined. When I think of my childhood, most of my memories are filled with my mother, as if my father never existed; he hardly features in them because my mother was so impactful in my life, always being present and selflessly catering for my and my sibling's needs. The problem is that women like my mother are often undermined because we've been misled to measure a woman's value by her economic success instead of the quality of life she so selflessly models for her children and husband. There's nothing wrong with a woman being a housewife as long as that decision is her own and is not made on her behalf.

Then there's the career woman who basically has her own career and is not reliant on men financially. She's often misconstrued as the woman who gave rise to the divorce rate. This woman wants a man who treats her the same way he wants to be treated; she wants a man who treats her as his equal. This woman is looking for love and intimacy in a relationship; she's not in it merely to survive. However, this is not as simple as it might sound. In most cases the aspects of homemaker and career woman co-exist in a woman. The difference is the focus each woman places on the two aspects of her personality. For example, you'll hardly find a career orientated woman who's not immersed in domestic life as well, even if it is peripheral to her main focus in life.

There's nothing wrong with being a man who prefers a housewife or a career woman, but there's a lot wrong with the notion that a woman can be nothing more than a housewife in a marriage. No woman is born a housewife, but men's expectations of their women can lead to them being just that even if that wasn't part of the woman's plans from the outset.

Much of my research for this book was based on men who are married to the latter — the career woman. I'm sure most men are familiar with women who are housewives, but many of us are still getting to know the latter. Marriage made me realize that a lot of what we men know about women is largely informed by patriarchy and not by women themselves. In conversations I had with my wife she said that she wanted to be more than just a wife or child bearer. She told me that before she was married, when she was with other women, the question she feared most was no longer "Are you married?" but rather "What do you do for a living?" This made me realize that most women today grow up yearning for independence and success, however once they get married they are advised to tone it down just a little bit to accommodate men who want a housewife rather than a career orientated woman.

I happen to be married to a woman who's independent and knows her worth, and in our marriage I try to break certain traditional and patriarchal notions that are rooted in the belief that a woman's place is in the kitchen. I would love for her to be part of the generation that says: "Beside (not behind) every successful man there's a successful woman." However sometimes she gets caught up in the web of patriarchy and societal pressure of what a woman's role is.

Here's one example: I prefer to iron my own clothes because, well, I'm really good at it (even in high school my mother had to cease ironing my uniform because she couldn't get my pleats right) and I enjoy doing it. One day while ironing my shirt my arm fell victim to its fiercely hot steel plate and left a burn mark. On our way to work that morning my wife asked me what I was going to tell people when they asked about the burn mark. "The truth, of course," I thought, but I then realized that within that question she was asking me to lie so that people wouldn't think of her as an incompetent wife. After all, what wife lets her man iron his own clothes? She knew they would ask.

This proves that our women are also trying to find their way in this new world where they are told that they are equal to men, but all of a sudden when they get married they are not as equal to men. At work they are expected to be domineering and ruthless like their male counterparts, but when they get home they should be submissive and caring; in business they are forced to adopt the masculine style of leadership, but they're expected to be more feminine at home. This is new to all of us.

What we must understand is that our generation is the testing ground for this world of equal partnership in marriage where both partners are providers and capable of leading. The ability of a woman to provide scares most men because our identity as men is derived from that role and when we realize that women can do that too our position as the head of the house feels threatened. As result we oppress our women and some men even use violence to show them who has more power in the relationship. As men we must understand that being a provider is what we do, not who we are. Your inability to provide shouldn't take away from your value and brilliance as a man. Once a person's value is based on their character, then no matter what role they may play in the relationship it will not have any impact on their value. This applies to men and women.

We must view our wives in a way that says their worth as human beings shouldn't be judged by their ability to cook or iron clothes. We should get to the point where a woman's character, attitude and the like are the yard stick to measure if she's wife material or not. Imagine if the only reason you're marrying her is because she's well domesticated, and then in the future you become rich and can basically afford to have a maid and cook in the house, what would become of your wife? What would make her wife material then?

However, in being equal both of you have to be in sync in defining and understand what that entails in your relationship. As much as you're equal, you are not the same (there's a catch to this — you should have seen it coming). Just as race cars on a track may possess the same power and potential, they have different designs. Our differences shouldn't be interpreted as one being better than the other. In his book, *Laugh Your Way to a Better Marriage*, Mark Gungor puts it this way: "...it is amazing how many men and women resist recognizing or discussing their differences. But these differences are the fingerprints of our gender. They are neither good nor bad, they are simply who we are. Birds fly, frogs croak, horses sleep standing up, and men and women do what they do. A loving intimate marriage relationship will leave room for gender differences without making the assumption that the other is wrong."

SHE'S HUMAN FIRST

"IN A LITERAL WAY MEN rule the world, and this made sense a thousand years ago because human beings lived then in a world in which physical strength was the most important attribute for survival. The physically stronger person was more likely to lead and men in general are physically stronger. Of course, there are many exceptions. But today we live in a vastly different world. The person more likely to lead is not the physically stronger person, it is the more creative person, the more intelligent person, the more innovative person, and there are no hormones for those attributes. A man is as likely as a woman to be intelligent, to be creative, to be innovative."

This is an excerpt from one of Chimamanda Ngozi Adichie's TED talks titled "We should all be feminists" that I came across on YouTube. I was hesitant to start the chapter this waybecause I feared that men, the people whom this book speaks to, would read it in defence mode and cease to engage with the rest of the book, especially since challenging the status quo makes most men uncomfortable. However, I chose to start with quoting her because for the first time ever in my life I recently got to understand how daily things which men see as insignificant can be so hurtful to women and impede their progress in life.

My wife and I went out on a date night, and after we had dinner, when it was time to pay, I realized that I didn't have my wallet with me. I panicked. My wife, Thuli (shout out, babes!), told me not to worry because she had her purse with her. She gave the waiter her card and, after inserting it into the Speed Point machine, the waiter came to my side of the table and handed me the machine to punch in the PIN. Bear in mind that this was Thuli's card which she had handed him. At the time we had the same PIN for both our cards (we have since changed that just so you know, scammers!) so I entered it into the machine.

I discussed the incident with Thuli but I didn't really see anything wrong with it, I just brushed it off as an innocuous mistake bythe waiter. It wasn't until I came across this TED talk a few days later that I understood how painful that experience was for her — the waiter (my brother in patriarchy) and I took away her right to use her own hard earned cash to pay for our meal. In a split second she was reduced to a mere wife who's dependent on her man. This TED talk helped me better understand women and the challenges they face on a daily basis.

Going back to the quote above, basically "back in the day" it was understandable to assume that men are superior to women because one's superiority was measured by physical strength. Today that is not the case. As men, it is important that we grasp this fact so that our own actions won't stifle the women we claim to love by putting them in a box that doesnot belong in this generation.

When people are dishing out marriage advice at a wedding reception a lot of emphasis is placed on infidelity, finances and other issues that are perceived to be the leading causes of divorce. But the most inconsequential things are the ones that usually build resentment that may actually result in a divorce. At my wedding, for example, no one talked about relationship dynamics when marrying a career woman. Not even one. And guess what *didn't* feature on the list of our problems in the following months? We had 99 problems, but infidelity and finance issues weren't among them. Instead we were fighting over my unrealistic expectations of her as a wife when we both have nine-to-five jobs.

I think the problem starts when we look at a woman and see a woman first instead of a human being. Back in varsity I shared a room with a friend who, to my advantage, happened to be a good cook. In order for him to be able to cook every day without complaining, I had to make sure that I washed the dishes and did the cleaning as well. These tasks were divided simply because it wouldn't have been fair of me to expect another human being to attend classes all day and do all the cooking and cleaning by themselves. However, when it comes to women, we men are trained to think they were designed for this and expect them to be able to go to work, then come back and clean the house, cook for us, feed and bathe the children, all while we nurse our backs and sore feet in front of the TV.

I must be honest, it took me an embarrassingly long two years of marriage and the birth of our son to realize that this "arrangement" was exhausting my wife, that she couldn't cope and, frankly, that no human should have to. What saddens me more is that she couldn't complain because, well, that's what was expected of her and I guess she thought I would think she was not cut out for marriage if she couldn't fulfil her "wifely duties".

I admit I'm a lazy man myself, and being the last born out of six children with three sisters didn't help either. My father, a hard-core Zulu man, was a traditionalist at heart and didn't want his boys to do "female" chores. I have all the excuses not to help out in the house and my culture supports this, but in this day and age I can't afford to have that mentality unless I take a wife who has personally chosen to live out her life as a housewife. And that is someone I can't afford. I mean I literally don't have the money to support that lifestyle, hence the reason for me writing this book.

On a serious note, though, challenging the status quo, at least one part of it, means that as a man you view your partner as a human being and not an object. If you view her as an object you're depriving yourself of an opportunity to grow and be challenged by another human being to be better than what you currently are. You are depriving your marriage of a beautiful, impregnable partnership that may help you achieve things you wouldn't have dreamed of before.

I personally feel like I would've had a better childhood or education had my mother been involved in how my father's income was spent; even knowing how much he earned would've had an impact. My dad took his own advice so seriously — never show your wife your pay slip — that he had to be assumed dead for a good three years of my tertiary education.

When I was filling in my NSFAS application forms to fund my tertiary education, one of the prerequisites was for my parents to go to the nearest police station and declare their combined income in an affidavit. This process, which should have been easy, was a problem for my dad because not only was he required to declare how much he earned, but he also had to produce his pay slip as proof. My dad was all for NSFAS and me getting a tertiary education until that very moment. Basically nothing in this life, even his son's education, would compel my dad to produce his pay slip; he hung on to it for dear life. My mom and I had to quickly hatch a plan: I would lie on the affidavit and say my father left us right after my birth and we didn't know if he was dead or alive. So I went to my dad and told him what we were thinking of doing, hoping that this proposed plan would hurt him and get him to change his mind. Guess what my dad said? As long as the plan didn't require him to produce his pay slip he was fine with it — we could even go as far as saying he was dead. *Thixo wase* George Goch!

This is what happens when one person is side-lined in a partnership. I mean why use one brain when you can use two? Wouldn't four legs help you reach your destination quicker than two? Wouldn't four eyes double your vision and make it clearer than two? In a team, when one of the team members is deprived of the opportunity to play and contribute it will affect the productivity of the entire team, not just the individual who's singled out. Imagine a goalie who's not allowed to move between the soccer goal posts — how is that goalie going to keep out goals from getting in? That team will lose every match even if it has the likes of Ronaldo and Messi upfront.

To have a marriage that is successful in all spheres of life is to live out FNB's tagline: "How can we help you?" However, the "we"must be replaced with "I". Always ask your partner what the best way is for you to support them.

I don't expect you, my fellow reader, to change the world; I don't expect you to march on the streets and *toyi-toyi* to challenge the status quo. I am not asking you to adopt a movement, however, you can change yourself and how you treat the women in your life. Marriage, after all, is a microcosm of society — an extension of you and your partner. Believe you me, the seeds you sow in your children shall not fall on barren ground.

BEFORE LOBOLO

WHAT YOU DO AND HOW you behave before tying the knot is of prime importance because there's no magical door that one goes through to cleanse oneself of any relationship vices and turn one into a perfect partner. In marriage there is no baptism that washes away the past. What your partner couldn't do before marriage they'll still fail to do once you're married — if she lacked respect before, marriage will not instil that in her, and if he was abusive or a serial cheater, marriage won't cure him.

There are some people who use marriage to bind them to their partner for life; they think marriage has some magical powers that will make any relationship issues they may have had in the past disappear. That's a myth. Marriage should be a confirmation of a decision already made; it is a manifestation of a bond that was created long before the question was popped. The "I do" vows that matter are not the ones you say in front of the pastor, but the ones you say to yourself, alone, with no pressure — the vows you say to yourself way before you even pop the question.

Marriage will not amplify adoration, reduce deep-seated feelings of resentment, erase fears of commitment or answer questions about whether or not this is the right move. Marriage is a ceremony that cements your current bond to another human being, and while that's a huge thing, that's all it does. Marriage will not change your spouse. It will not make her more mature, more loyal to you, or more respectful. How your partner treats you before lobolo is how they will treat you once you are married, and to assume otherwise is setting yourself up for failure. Likewise, marriage will not change you.

The first thing that's important to know before you commit to "until death do us part" is the type of person your partner is. Observe how your partner treats her parents when she's annoyed. In the early stages of a relationship new love has a way of ensuring we're on our best behaviour. The love we feel inside conceals who we really are. If you are normally impatient then you suddenly have an abundance of patience; if you are used to going out every weekend, you suddenly enjoy being indoors with your partner. Until, of course, the infatuation wears off and the act of loving begins. It is important to know how she treats her parents — the people she holds dear to her heart — because that is an indication of how she'll treat you down the line.

The sad reality is that after some time your partner will get to the same level of familiarity with you as she has with her parents, and in that space of comfort one's true character will resurface. The surfacing of their true character is not a bad thing, the issue is whether you were aware of it before and whether or not you can tolerate it.

One mistake people should never make is marrying someone with the hope of fixing them; if you do that it should be a clear choice you've made.

There were many things that my father failed to do for his children that gradually ate away the respect that I had for him. However, once I reached adulthood I quickly realized that my disrespectful approach wouldn't work if I wanted to get through to him. I had to respect him even when I felt there was no reason for that simply because he was my father. If it was any other man, regardless of the age difference, I would have given him the same level of respect, or lack thereof, that he gave me. However, because a relationship between a child and parent often defies the rules that govern human interaction, it demands that we forgive without an apology and love even when it is unreciprocated. In the same way in a marriage there will come a point where as the man, you'll have to love a disrespectful wife and the wife will, at some point, have respect for her unloving husband.

When we're hurt we often want nothing more than to inflict the same level of pain on the perpetrator; it takes a certain level of maturity to know that doing what is right doesn't necessarily mean acting according to how you feel. What would a woman achieve by being disrespectful to her man when he's committed an act that she perceives as being disrespectful to her? What would a woman achieve by cheating on her man after finding out that he's been unfaithful to her? It's therefore important to know how she treats her parents when there's no reason for her to be civil or respectful.

On their blog PreEngaged.com a married couple, Heather and Eric, write the following: "Gentlemen, she may be gorgeous, sweet, and treat you like the entire world revolves around you, but if she treats her dad with disrespect; if she whines and complains to him and about him; if she treats him like an ATM and does not honour him as the head of her house, it is only a matter of time before she will treat you the same way."

This is, however, tricky to assess if you're a black South African because chances are you'll only get to meet your in-laws during or after the lobolo negotiations. African families hardly ever invite boyfriends to dinners and lunches and that is the situation I found myself in when I met my wife. I couldn't go to any intimate family function with her while I was still her boyfriend; I had to support her from a distance.

Back then I was living in a flat in Jo'burg CBD and she was staying at home in Vereeniging. Being a guy, I would always push my luck whenever she was around and ask her to spend the night at my place. She always refused, even when I tried to use emotional blackmail. Thuli had so much respect for her mother that she would risk breaking up with me instead of disobeying her mother, even though she was over 21 — *uGogo-ongaka* as they'd say in the township.

I did get my way at times, but the work that went into lying to her mother was unbelievable. I remember this one time when we were celebrating one year of being together and Thuli promised me that we would spend the weekend together. "But how?" I asked. "Trust me, *babakhe*, I've got this," she said. The lying that went into making that weekend happen shocked even me.

Thuli had asked one of her friends to call her when she was at home with her mother and pretend to be a potential employer who was calling all the applicants who'd been short listed for interviews which would take place on the following Monday morning at their Jo'burg offices. The friend even sent an SMS with the interview details with emphasis placed on arrival time which was 7:00am. For the next 15 minutes or so Thuli and her mother wracked their brains trying to figure out how she was going to get there on time since Vereeniging is so far from Jo'burg and they didn't want to risk her getting there late.

At the time Thuli had a friend named Becca (the very same friend who made the call and sent the SMS), who lived in the varsity res and Thuli's mother knew that they were best friends. It came as no surprise when Thuli suggested that it might be better if she spent the night at Becca's since she stayed in Jo'burg. Her mother agreed, saying "Why didn't we think of that in the first place?" While they were still in that joyful spirit Thuli took advantage of the situation and told her mom that in order to sleep at the res one must physically go to their offices and apply for permission to sleep over. The only problem, though, Thuli lamented, was that their offices weren't open on weekends. That meant that she had to go there on Friday and stay with Becca until the day of the interview. Her mom responded, "No problem, Mtanami, please make sure you leave early on Friday just in case there's queues." My poor mother-in-law; she wouldn't have been impressed to know that the "interview" was at my place.

As much as I was shocked by Thuli's scheming, my admiration and love for her grew because of the way she treats her mother. (Her father passed away when she was in her early teens). I didn't really know what it meant back then, but now I understand why she respects me even when she's annoyed. (I hope I'm not jinxing it!)

The second important thing at this stage of the relationship is to know yourself and observe your father or the man who filled a father figure role in your life, because our parents are our main role models for relationships. This is not to say that just because someone's parents have a dysfunctional relationship he or she is doomed to repeat the parents' mistakes, but the norms created by our parents' relationships do follow us into our own. Marriage coaching is a good place to address these potential problems before marriage.

Growing up I never saw my father washing dishes or cleaning the house or even making his own bed for example, it was always my mother who did those things. My dad never really did any chores in the house and nobody complained because my parents were happy with that arrangement (or maybe not — I should probably ask my mom). I was the same in the early days of our marriage, forgetting that my wife, unlike my mother, has a nine-to-five job and, more than that, she'd appreciate a man who helps around in the house.

The next thing one must do is to envision the big picture of your married self. What kind of a husband do you want to be? What kind of a lover do you want to be? What kind of a partner do you want to be? Goals will emerge from those answers. These goals will help you be the man in that big picture. For example, if you have a goal to be a better listener, then working on your listening skills on a daily basis will make you a better listener over time, and if being a good listener means being a good husband as you had envisioned, then this too will become true. The image of you as a husband should be there before you even decide to pop the question. What you aspire to be will help you take the right path even when your heart says otherwise. When challenges come, for they will come, they test one's character and will power. If you don't define the type of man you want to be circumstances will decide that for you.

Throughout this process you should also scrutinize the people who first taught you about marriage — most likely your parents. Look at the negative character traits that you might need to work on to break the cycle. For example, I don't drink alcohol, and this is not because I'm a staunch Christian or because the Holy Ghost has been guiding me all my life. I basically grew up in a household where alcohol wasn't prevalent. My parents didn't have to tell me that alcohol is bad for me, but they created an environment where it was normal not to drink — this was way before I even knew that drinking alcohol is a sin to many Christians. My point is that whatever our parents model to us, whether good or bad, may become a norm in our lives.

If your father constantly criticized and hurled insults at your mother you're most likely to do that to your partner. Why? Because, as stated in Gary Chapman's book *Things I wish I'd known Before We Got Married*, "We have grown up with our parents; we don't recognize their patterns of communication as being unhealthy. For us, it is simply the way it has always been. It often takes someone outside the family drawing the communication pattern to our attention to help us understand why the pattern needs to be changed. Because we are influenced by our parents' communication patterns, we are very likely to adopt them as our own."

Obviously this is not confined to communication, but also applies to other areas that may affect the way you treat your partner. It is important for you to identify these traits (with the help of your partner who would have noticed them by now) and seek professional counselling to help you break the bad pattern. It would be naïve of us to think we don't come into a relationship with baggage that may cause problems, so be honest with yourself and work on those traits that may be a threat to your relationship.

A friend of mine recently told me how he despised his father who had two wives and failed to take care of his children. He made a promise to himself when he got married that he would be everything that his late father was not — a loving and faithful husband to his wife. Unfortunately he did not get the necessary help to break the pattern, and he only managed to keep his word for two years of their marriage. In the third year he fell in love with another woman and three years later they had a child together. To this day, six years later, they are still together and the first wife has accepted the situation — he basically has two wives now.

This is a man who started off with good intentions, but sadly it turned out that the fruit doesn't fall too far from the tree. Something happened in that third year of his marriage that changed this man; there was a battle inside him that lasted for God knows how long, and by not dealing with that original *trait* he ended up following the leading of his body instead of doing the right thing.

    Chances are he would have dealt with it better from the beginning had he taken the correct steps in dealing with his past and unlearned the lessons about marriage that were first taught to him by his parents. This would have helped him to be better prepared and have a support structure in place (be it a friend or marriage coach) that would ensure he did not turn out like his father. However, because he was so fixated on the past he forgot to deal with the present.

BUILDING A SUPPORT STRUCTURE

When you say to a woman, "I want to spend the rest of my life with you," you surely don't mean that you want to hurt her, cheat on her, make her contemplate her relationship status on Facebook or make her life a living hell. You don't mean that, but most men end up doing just that. Not because they've initially set out to be like that, but because circumstances, societal pressure, the lack of knowledge of self and challenges will sweep you away like a strong current if you are not standing on firm ground. However even if you are standing on firm ground, you can't stand alone — there must be a group of men around you to serve as a support structure.

I like the idea used by Alcoholics Anonymous of having a sponsor to help recovering alcoholics. A sponsor is an individual who is there to offer guidance and support to the recovering alcoholic or sponsee. This is one of the most powerful tools to help people stay sober in AA. The sponsor is not only the person who guides the member through the AA program, but is also there to listen. Being able to rely on an empathetic ear can be particularly important when the individual feels on the verge of relapse. This, I believe, is a structure that the current generation of men can create to help every man out there to remain faithful and committed to their partner and marriage. It's not that men are all irresponsible and need to be kept on a leash for them to behave, it's just that, as Jesus said in Matthew 26:41, the spirit is indeed willing but the flesh is weak. The sponsor will therefore come in handy when *inyama ifuna okwayo*.

One of your goals as a man should be to have such men in your life. Whether you seek them through marriage seminars or at church is up to you, but having this support structure is crucial. The problem with modern society is that when men seek help it's seen as a sign of weakness, whereas it should be perceived as a sign of strength because to build is to fortify. However, if we continue with the notion of *indoda-ayikhali* and believe we're immune to life's challenges and temptations we'll continue breeding the same type of men that we have vowed *not* to become. To avoid falling into the same trap we need to reconsider our approach to marriage. As a man you need like-minded people who will help you weather the storms when they come.

So many odds are stacked against married men these days. When you go on social media you'll hardly find any inspiring stories about married men; all one hears is how promiscuous and abusive they are. If that's the only information you consume on a daily basis, soon you'll end up believing that's the norm and will make it your reality. Nothing will inspire you to do better because you would have been led to believe that all married men are like that — they don't have self-control or can't control their tempers. And once you entertain such thoughts it's only a matter of time before they manifest in your life and become a reality you can't get yourself out of.

So, as men, as much as we are strong and determined to see through whatever we have started, maybe it's time we admit that certain things can't be achieved by one man alone but need a team. Only a naïve person would think that they'd spend approximately 40 years in marriage and in all that time not have any moments of weakness or lack of willpower. So, in your efforts to be a good husband don't forget to surround yourself with good men who'll give you sound advice when the going gets tough.

WORK, WORK, WORK!

Most men only want the benefits of marriage but not the hard work that comes with it. In fact, it is your responsibility as a man to do exactly what you mean when you say "I want to spend the rest of my life with you", which is to take good care of her. It doesn't have to be Hollywood perfect, but it has to be enough for her.

Take care of your woman not out of fear that you might lose her to another man, but rather because it is your responsibility to do so. Responsibility simply means doing what is expected of you — your duty. I think the real problem with men today is that we've been spoiled into thinking that by taking good care of our women we're simply doing them a favour. We've forgotten that most women don't marry to survive anymore; they also choose to be with us as much as we asked for their hand in marriage.

So why should it be a woman's duty to be caring, honest, trustworthy and committed but not ours? I understand that mentality from back in the day because the societal structures were set up in a way that would allow women to offer nothing other than themselves and the qualities listed above, but now they work just as much as men and bring in just as much money. I'm not trying to romanticize this or be politically correct, I just know how "chilled" we men are when it comes to relationships. That's not because men are callous, but because as men we are generally content with the state of the relationship and don't fancy the idea of working on it — we prefer watching sports over spending quality time with our partner, for example.

However, women are wired differently; women are not as easily satisfied with the state of the relationship. David Roadhouse, a Chicago psychotherapist, suggested the reason for the disparity might be that "on the whole, men experience fulfilment more easily than women do. Women are filled with all these romantic yearnings and romance is finite, limited, difficult to sustain." Be that as it may, we must attend to our partner's needs if we want to have a good relationship. It's not easy, and no one said it would be, but with the right motivation and good men around you no mountain should be too high to climb.

To take it a step further, working on one's marriage is not enough; one needs the right tools as well. In the words of Mark Gungor: "The thing that makes marriage wonderful is work. But we need more than just work; we need skill. Just because we are willing to work for a great marriage does not mean we have the skills to pull one off. Those skills take time and knowledge. The longer we wait to learn those skills, the more apt we are to tumble from one painful relationship to another." When the honeymoon phase fades you'll be faced with this: work.

It's not as taxing as I make it sound — or maybe it is — but at the end of the day it's worth it. In the early months of our marriage Thuli and I used to fight a lot because I have this habit or *umkhuba* (sounds more accurate in Zulu) of not calling her to let her know that I arrived safely whenever I visit friends or get to work. I didn't understand why she got upset over such a little thing, but it meant a lot to her. I tried to explain to her that it's not that I intentionally didn't listen to her, it's just I was not used to doing that and my family could vouch for me — I'm that person who doesn't call when I get to my destination.

However, in the end it didn't matter how many genuine excuses I had or how I felt about it, the bottom line was that it made her upset and the only way to change that was for me to work on it. I went as far as setting a reminder on my phone just in case I forgot to call her when I got to work. It started as a strenuous activity, but over time it became a daily routine and now it's natural — although I sometimes still forget occasionally when I'm with my friends. I chose to listen to my wife and work on the problem and it made a big difference in our relationship.

WHAT MEN THINK WOMEN WANT

'LL START THIS OFF BY saying that my opinion on this subject is informed by a little survey I did with married men although they didn't know that I was conducting research. It is said that a drunk man tells no tales, so the study was done in a casual way to ensure respondents did not give rehearsed answers but rather honest ones, encouraged by a glass of wine or two. I'm not claiming to actually know what goes on in the minds of women, however the similarities in the answers I got when I asked husbands what they thought their wives wanted led to these deductions.

You'll note that I often quote Mark Gungor, the author of *Laugh Your Way to a Better Marriage,* and that's because I think he's one of the few honest authors who do not romanticize the realities that married couples face. In his blog, The Mark Gungor Show, he says: "If you ask women to describe their ideal man, many will describe a man who loves to converse and open up. They want someone who enjoys the little details of life, someone who remembers all the things that are important to them, and someone who would rather share with them about the day than stare at the TV all night." In the end he concludes by saying that women seem to want a girlfriend type of man. And that is not possible. There are certain things that men may try to work on to make their wives happy, but most of the time we just revert to who we are: being glued to the TV and asked to do something a thousand times before we do it.

Below are four things that all the men I've engaged with touched on in terms of what they think their wives want ...

1. A ROMANTIC MAN (almost every day)

This is a tricky one, because as much as we might say it's unrealistic to expect a husband to be romantic every day, at some point in the beginning of the relationship we made it seem like it was possible. During the honeymoon phase your girlfriend is the first thing you think of in the morning and the last thing on your mind in the evening. You'd call her every now and then, and at night, depending on which network you use, you'd talk until the early hours of the morning. You'd go as far as learning how to cook just so you could make her supper or breakfast in bed. In this stage being a romantic comes naturally.

According to Mark Gungor, it is this stage of the relationship that convinces us that the other person is the "one" — a stage which can be deceitful and misguiding. In this stage she has all your attention. However, that stage wears off, and once you're married your attention shifts to your career, debit orders, in-laws, children, and the other things that fill our lives. There is no longer any need for courtship — or so we think.

In this stage, as noted by Gary Chapman, author of *The Five Love Languages*, routine and resentment can silently eat away at the love that you once had. In this stage lovers can become enemies, not because you lied to trick your woman into marriage, but because at that moment in time you were genuine in how you felt and in the way you treated her but it was an unrealistic standard that was set up for failure. The infatuation in the honeymoon phase borders on obsession and is different from what comes thereafter — real love. What you feel in both the honeymoon phase and thereafter is genuine, but infatuation is inferior simply because in this phase there's nothing a man cares about other than the idea of his partner. A man loses interest in other things, even his job or business, and I'm pretty sure that no woman wants a man who's got nothing but love to offer.

2. A MAN WHOSE BEST FRIEND IS HIS WIFE

Women like the idea of being married to their best friend. They don't understand how you could consider another guy your best friend when they're by your side. Being best friends with your spouse may look good on a Facebook post or Instagram, but realistically speaking it's a burden. You can't fulfil all her emotional needs, just like she can't fulfil all yours. Some of that burden must be shared by family and friends. If you think you can be your wife's best friend, you're mistaken. And that doesn't mean your marriage isn't wonderful, it's just important to recognize that friendship and marriage, while they share key areas of overlap, are fundamentally different relationships. And conflating the two can cause far more problems for your marriage, experts warn. In most cases our friends do not live with us and are not financially, legally or relationally entwined with us. Our friends are attached to us because they want to be, when they want to be, they have volition and empowerment to leave or at least take space from us when necessary. Our partners are inextricably connected to our homes, family, schedules and life.

Husbands who expect their wives to be their best friends may develop impractical expectations of how they should support them and their decisions. If a man were to quit his job to pursue a passion, for example, a friend could easily be his cheerleader. But his wife? She's going to have questions.

I don't know how, but women have a way of making men lose interest in other friendships outside marriage. Most men fall into this trap and become over dependent on their partner to a point that they become control freaks, checking on them every minute whenever they are away from each other.

Let's go back to the beginning of the relationship and see what attracted you guys to each other. The long conversations that you had while staring into each other's eyes were not due to either of you being good orators, but because you two led different, interesting lives and it was exciting to hear about your individual lives and the silly things you got up to with your friends. However, if you now allow the monotonous coexistence to define your marriage at the expense of individual growth and fulfilment, you suck the passion and fire out of it.

It's important to have a friendship and do things together as a couple, but it's equally important to have friends outside of marriage and be an individual. If you don't have your own likes, interests and hobbies, it becomes difficult to give your partner someone unique and exciting with whom to connect and fall in love with repeatedly. Give yourself permission to have your own interests outside of your relationship; it not only helps you, it also helps your relationship.

Give each other space. At times when you are experiencing problems in your marriage you'll find that they can't be resolved through conversing but rather by your absence. When you have some space to think you can gain a different perspective and have time for introspection. That space rejuvenates you and makes you appreciate your partner even more because when you are away from her you are able to see your marriage from a spectator's perspective and may realize that whatever you are arguing about is really not such a big issue.

3. A MAN WHO HAS THE RIGHT KIND OF FRIENDS

Now let's turn our focus to the issue of friends. I don't want to sound biased, so let's get this out of the way — some friends can be misleading and bad for you, that is a fact. So, when you're married, what type of friends are you allowed to keep? Most people would say friends who are also married or engaged, just like Christians would keep friends who are also Christians to avoid any who might be a bad influence. However, this would mean that if you had a friend who's married and after a few years he gets divorced your friendship ends there just because he's now single. That's a flawed way of thinking; you can't choose friends based on their relationship status but rather on their character.

So what I'm basically saying is that you can have a married friend who doesn't respect the sanctity of marriage or have a friend who's single but respects and believes in the sanctity of marriage. And by single I don't mean single-single, I mean he's not married but has someone he's in a long-term relationship with or *bayakipita*. To tell you the truth, a single-single friend is a problem; their version of a relationship is not good for you. You won't relate when it comes to women and they will continually tell you that you're being controlled by your wife. No matter how long you've been friends, once one of you gets married and the other continues with his two minute-long relationship, your conversation on relationships will be the end of the friendship. So the trick is not only to have friends who are married, but also friends who have the same attitude towards marriage as you.

Lastly, be sure to differentiate between friends who will add value to your relationship and the ones who subtract from it; differentiate between the ones who will remind you of the reason why you got married and the ones who will remind you what you are missing out on in life by being married. Married men can be poisonous too, and it may be hard to detect the negatives in what they say and do because you don't expect that from them, so one must be careful in choosing who to hang out with.

4. CLOSE TO NO RELATIONSHIP WITH THE IN-LAWS

If you come from a traditional family, the way most African families are in South Africa, where a *makoti* is expected to perform certain *makoti* duties whenever she's at her husband's parents' house, you'll be lucky to find a *makoti* who's happy with her in-laws. However, the *makoti* and in-laws' rivalry is very complex and needs a book on its own, so I'll just mention it in brief.

Essentially there is the guy's mother who wants to continue loving and protecting her son (especially from the new daughter in-law who's a stranger to her) and then there's the wife who is doing the same thing — trying to protect her husband from people she perceives as leeches who are always asking for money or the like. Our wives will never see our parents or family the way we do. Where I think my mother is caring, my wife may think she's overbearing. When she's being helpful to me, she maybe seen as trying to show my wife how inept she is at taking care of her son. This is a constant struggle.

The process of a man separating from his family is rushed by most wives. They put their man in a dilemma where he has to choose between his family and his wife. In her blog, Dienna Brann writes that: "If you think about your husband for a minute, you can see he is in a precarious situation. He loves his parents because, well... they are his parents; but he loves you because you are you and you make him feel loved in a way no else has done. He chose you to be the person with whom he wants to spend his life. Sometimes this idea — his choosing you because he loves you and wants to spend his life with you — gets forgotten or lost. Sometimes you see his behaviour and feel uncomfortable because you're not sure how important you really are to him."

Please, if you are a man reading this book, show your woman this passage. It may take some time for the separation process to take place, but not the eternity some men allow it to stretch to. I personally believe that a man who's easily separated from his family by his wife or girlfriend may be led to do the same to his wife by a *makhwapheni* or bad influence, but that's just me.

In trying to maintain a good relationship between wife and in-laws, the rule on the streets is this: Don't bad mouth your wife to your family. Let her flaws and arguments be known to you and only you. That's because as her husband you can easily forgive and forget, but your family will not be as kind, and families have an elephant's memory when it comes to a *makoti'* s mistakes. Even after ten years you'll hear them murmur "*okusalayo*", and we all know no good is uttered after that phrase.

RELATIONSHIP / MARRIAGE

AS AN INDIVIDUAL YOU CONSTANTLY set goals for your life because you know that to achieve something one has to plan and put effort into taking steps that will help one reach those goals. This is vital to being successful at whatever you do because success doesnot happen by chance. A relationship also functions like that, but how many of us actually take some time out to set relationship goals or have a realistic vision of the type of relationship we want?

In his book, *Things I Wish I'd Known Before We Got Married*, Gary Chapman puts it like this: "What is ironic is that we recognize the need for education in all other pursuits of life and fail to recognize that need when it comes to marriage. Most people spend far more time in preparation for their vocation than they do in preparation for marriage. Therefore, it should not be surprising that they are more successful in their vocational pursuits than they are in reaching the goal of marital happiness."

In our society men are taught to think that the important part of the relationship is *ukushela* and that's where all the hard work goes into. After the courting it's retirement — you stop working and let her do all the work. And that is not how it is supposed to be. If anything, courtship is a breeze and more work should be put into the relationship after you're married; neither of you should relax. Work on looking good for your partner like you did when you were still asking her out; continue to make her feel special and good about herself.

In the past when I heard someone say "work on looking good for your partner" I'd roll my eyes and say things like, "I'm used to her, so even if she can rock a Riana hair style nothing will change." But I was wrong. One day my wife rocked up with a razor cut which was completely out of character and daring because she usually plays it safe when it comes to hair styles. But that hairstyle did something to me; I guess I never expected it, and all the dormant demons that lay inside me were suddenly evoked. Sometimes it's not even a hair style but her zest for life or intelligence during a conversation that will awaken that tiger in you. The point is, work on yourself, both internally and externally.

A word of warning: You cannot make your marriage successful on your own, but you can break your relationship single-handedly.

Most often we men come into relationships full of expectations, forgetting that our women have their own expectations as well. Setting goals for your relationship will help you as a man enter your marriage with one hand full of expectation and the other with stuff to offer your wife. When you take your relationship seriously and make plans for how to keep the love burning that will also motivate your partner without you having to say a word to her. When you have a blueprint of what you want your relationship to be it becomes easier to build because you will focus your energy on meaningful things.

For example, I grew up in a home where my parents hid their conflict from us children. We could sense the tension between them but we never heard any shouting (well, maybe a little from my mother) or insults being hurled around us. I liked that and told myself that when I got married I would treat conflicts between my wife and I the same way. So I practiced that — whenever I'm in a heated argument with my wife I make sure that I don't use any insults or derogatory words, no matter how angry I may be. (I must admit though it's not as easy as my dad made it seem.) Nothing justifies a man putting his hand on his woman, nor should anger justify me hurling expletives at my wife.

One thing I've realized is that because I don't do that to her when we fight, she doesn't do it to me either, no matter how much I've wronged her. This didn't happen miraculously, though, it's part of the plan for our marriage and I had to be the person who deals with conflict gracefully before I asked her to do the same. I have plans for what I want my marriage to be like and this makes it easier for me to pick out things that are not part of the plan when we have arguments. When my voice escalates during arguments she'll say *ungangithethisi* and I'll quickly apologize and lower my voice (I'm not sure about the apologizing part from me though) because shouting at each other is not part of my plans for our marriage. Having plans for your marriage will make it easy for you to pick out meteorites that don't belong in the world that you're creating with your partner.

Sir Isaac Newton's third law of motion states that for every action there's an equal and opposite reaction. However, in most relationships, people go about it the wrong way — they expect good results without putting in any effort. They sit and hope that by some chance the relationship will remain exciting and fun. That's a terrible strategy.

There are two kinds of men in the world today — those who care a lot about what other men think of them and those who only care about what their woman thinks of them. The first type are the guys who don't want to be perceived as being too romantic or loving because other guys will think *"udlisiwe"* or, simply put, "not MAN enough". Too many men seek to please their friends at the expense of their partners.

This is not all their own fault, though. Let me side track a little bit here — peer pressure among men is real! When men are hanging out together the only stories that get applause are those of them mistreating their partner or "putting her in her place". It's hard for men to be good husbands and still get respect from their peers. Some women will also burn you at the stake for being loving and loyal to your partner. They won't say it explicitly, but you'll hear comments such as "You love your woman way too much" or *"bakufakele ikorobela"*.

The second type are the guys who put their woman's happiness first before anything else, they don't care about their friends' approval or being called a "sissy"; as long as their partner is happy they are happy. The issue with this, though, is that some men end up being a woman's puppet, lonely and with no friends. In township lingo when this occurs, we say *ukudonsangekhala.* In the end you must often choose between getting your friends' approval and having a happy partner; you can't have both simultaneously. This becomes a constant struggle in a relationship and one must find a balance between the two. However, this needn't be a struggle if your partner genuinely feels like she comes first before your friends. When she has that assurance from you she'll easily give you the "visa" to go and see your friends.

After we've been married a while we easily forget that our wives made a lot of sacrifices to be with us. They bought into our vision, changed their last name and moved in with us because they love us and want what is best for us. When they call out certain habits or caution us about the friends we keep we often see it as controlling instead of a genuine concern from their side. One thing you must know, though, is that no one else has your best interests at heart more than your wife, so you should put her first 95% of the time (the other 5% is for friends and family). After all, you are the one who asked her to be your wife.

LOVE

"LOVE IS A FORCE GENERATED by a decision. Love has no feelings you know. If God responded to you the way he felt about what you did to him you wouldn't be redeemed today. You see, this is important because true love has no feelings — it's a choice. Remember now feelings are chemicals and chemicals change every five minutes, so if I love you because I feel like I love you, you might lose your love in five minutes. Ever heard this: 'We fell out of love'; or 'We don't love each other anymore'? What that means is that the chemicals changed. '...the way I used to feel when I looked at you, you don't look that way no more, so I don't get the feeling no more. You're bigger, fatter, heavier. You changed on me after five children, you don't look the same.' Love is a choice, you choose to love. Love is an act of will. We keep thinking that love is some emotional contortion deep in the soul. Love is an act of will. You can decide to love your enemy... how can you do that? It has to be a decision. That's the kind of love you need for marriage because the person in your marriage will be an enemy twice a week or maybe twice a day."

This is an excerpt from one of Dr Myles Munroe's talks on YouTube titled *Misunderstanding Love: part 1*. What struck me about it is the fact that he talks about the kind of love that people don't want to hear about but which they will inevitably encounter because that is the reality of love in a marriage.

The biggest misconception about love is that it is devoid of pain and suffering. Once a person gets hurt in a relationship, love is called into question. After talking to men who are in toxic relationships, men who've had to plead with another man to stop sleeping with their wives, men who've been cheated on while cheating as well, and men who are in bitter and unhappy marriages but still claim to love their wives, I realized that love is more than a feeling. Love is a choice — you wake up every day and choose to love your spouse unconditionally.

When you get married you make a vow to the one you love that you'll be by their side and true to them in good and bad times, for richer and for poorer. Bad times or poorer times do not inspire romance do they? We all want to experience the good times but not the bad ones. Sometimes the bad times can suck out the warmth and happiness in a marriage, killing all the hopes you might have had for a happy marriage. But they are nothing more than a season that will pass in time, a chapter in your marriage journey. That's why people stay even when it hurts — not because they can't breathe without the other person, but because they've made a decision that although seasons may come and go and feelings may change, they will continue to love this person.

Generally my wife and I are very loving and have a beautiful marriage; I couldn't have asked for a better partner. However, we sometimes have days where there's constant fighting over little things (I may be trivializing issues because I'm always the perpetrator).

Sometimes I'll be driving home from work and I think that maybe it will be better if I pass by certain friends and stay longer to avoid the issues brewing at home. I know I'll find the comforting words "Wives can be nagging" in any group of men I might detour to. But then again it hits me that as much as every fibre of my body doesn't want to face the furnace awaiting me at home, is it really a good decision to stay away? Is it a good decision to run away from an issue regardless of who's in the wrong? What solution would my absence bring?

I then make a decision right there and then that as much as we are fighting, and as much as I'm not Thuli's favourite person at the moment, I need to go home and love my wife in an unloving environment. I choose to go and face the music, knowing that whatever we may be facing at that moment doesn't define our marriage and that there will always be a light at the end of the tunnel.

However, this outcome doesn't depend solely on me. Thuli also has a choice to pack up and go or pack up all my belongings and kick me out of the house. But she doesn't do any of those things; instead she waits for me to return from work so that we can fix our marriage. She chooses to wait for me because she loves me in spite of our situation at the time. I often picture her sitting on the couch watching TV while waiting for me thinking *"uzong'tholakahle lo today!"* But she loves me nonetheless.

People who believe that love is all about feelings and butterflies in the stomach don't last in relationships because as soon as the butterflies migrate or feelings change they want to leave the marriage. For them it is all about what the heart wants. They forget that throughout history and in the Bible as well we've learned that there's nothing as deceitful as a human heart. No passage echoes this better than Jeremiah 17:9 where it says "the heart is deceitful above all things and desperately wicked". I've learned that in marriage taking the decision to love unconditionally will channel your heart onto the right path.

In choosing to love our partners we must also express our love in a way that will be meaningful to them; in other words, scratch where it itches. You can only do that if you understand your spouse's love language. I'll explore this more in the next chapter.

LOVE MEETS RELATIONSHIP

IN HIS BOOK *START WITH Why*, Simon Sinek says this about the human limbic system; it is "the part of the brain that controls our feelings [and] has no capacity for language. It is this disconnection that makes putting our feelings into words so hard. We have trouble, for example, explaining why we married the person we married. We struggle to put into words the reasons why we love them, so we talk around it or rationalize it. 'She's funny, she's smart,' we start. But there are lots of funny and smart people in the world, but we don't love them or want to marry them." (Before you run to the bookstore to buy the book I thought you should know that it's not about marriage — not even close.)

So how then can your partner know that you love them if, by nature, you can't put it into words? The simple answer would be to just show them. Love is communicated thoroughly through actions which give birth to a relationship. In most townships a kiss or *lamza* marks the beginning of the relationship. A relationship is not love, instead it is a method people employ to show their love for one another, and therefore becomes a yardstick to judge whether your partner really, really loves you. She can only feel loved if you act lovingly, and for your acts of love to have the desired effect, as a man you must understand which acts of love resonate with your partner.

I recently came across a book by Gary Chapman which talks about the five love languages. The book is based on the simple premise that people speak different love languages. For your partner to feel loved that love must be communicated to her in a language that she understands. No matter how much you try to express your love in isiZulu, if your woman only understands Venda she'll never feel loved. In the same way Gary Chapman breaks love languages into five categories — five ways in which people speak and understand love:

- *Words of Affirmation:* Using words that build her up or words of appreciation. Words of affirmation include encouraging words, kind words and humble words.

- *Quality Time:* This simply means giving your partner undivided attention with the TV off or devices down, looking at each other and talking. Quality time calls for sympathetic listening with the view to understanding your partner's thoughts and feelings. Quality time also includes quality activities which basically means doing something together that will make your partner feel loved and cared for.

- *Receiving Gifts:* A gift is a symbol of a thought; it says "I'm thinking about you even when you are not with me." It is not only the thought implanted in the mind that counts, but even more importantly the thought expressed in the act of actually securing the gift and giving it as an expression of love; gifts are visual symbols of love. However, there's an intangible gift that sometimes speaks more loudly than a gift that can be held in one's hand, and that is the gift of presence — being there when your partner needs you.

- *Acts of Service:* This means doing things you know your partner would like you to do. You simply seek to please her by serving her, to express your love for her by doing things for her. This can include cooking, cleaning the house, changing the baby's diaper, etc. which are all acts of service. These acts will require some of us to re-examine our stereotypes of the roles of husbands and wives.

- *Physical Touch:* This is also a powerful vehicle for communicating love. Holding hands, kissing, embracing and sexual intercourse are all ways of communicating love to your partner. Love touches may be explicit and demand your full attention, such as in a back rub or foreplay, culminating in intercourse, but love touches may also be implicit and require only a moment, such as putting your hand on her shoulder as you pour a cup of coffee or rubbing your body against hers as you pass in the kitchen.

Discovering the primary love language of your partner is important if you want to keep her love tank full. It is essential for you as a man to get this right in your marriage so that your acts of love won't be like water off a duck's back. I know most men will struggle with acts of service because of culture. As a Zulu man myself, the notion of even knowing where the broom is kept is frowned upon. However, culture evolves and so do marriages. The only thing that seems to remain static is patriarchy.

When this topic comes up during conversations with other men either at work or church, every man will deny doing any acts of service for his partner. I have one particular friend who is hell bent on maintaining the status quo when it comes to the traditional roles of husbands and wives. As we all know, in every group of friends there's always one who has a harder personality than the rest of us; the one who's just too quick to get into fights. This friend of mine is that guy. Whenever we talk about babies and changing diapers he's adamant that he'll never do that; he says his wife knows that and doesn't bother him with it. You can imagine the admiration on the faces of the other men and the pride he feels looking down on us diaper-changing men.

However, one day his wife invited my wife and me to lunch at their place on a Saturday. The food was delicious and we were having a great time. Since they have more kids than us, my wife asked my friend's wife how they cope with so many kids. My friend's wife happily admitted that they area handful but, fortunately for her, her husband helps her with the kids. "Like how?" I interjected before she could finish talking. "Like feeding the kids and changing their diapers every now and then when I'm tired," she continued.

You should have seen the glee on my face in that moment. If you gave me a million rand I still wouldn't have the same glee I felt that day watching my friend shrink and squirm in his seat. This is part of toxic masculinity and one of the ways in which patriarchy is harmful to men — men give the impression that they haven't changed with the times when in reality most of us have but won't admit it in front of our peers because of the fear of being perceived as less of a man.

Don't be fooled by street talk, always do what is best for your marriage, and in this case it is discovering what your partner's love language is and communicating your love for her effectively.

TOXIC MASCULINITY

THE PROBLEM WITH MY FRIEND who lied about not helping around in the house is that he viewed taking care of his kids domestically as something that would make him lose his manhood among his peers, so he felt he had to lie. This is the challenge that many men face today — we lead double lives; we say one thing around friends and act differently at home.

One of the attributes of being a man is courage, but somehow we have none of that when we are around other men. We'd rather lie about who we are at home just so we don't lose our status among friends. In many groups this is taken to extremes because it extends to domestic violence where men glorify the perpetrators of the abuse and condone their violence just to fit in.

Let me recount a story that left me with my jaw on the floor. One day after church a group of guys was sitting together casually talking about life. Naturally the conversation then moved to us talking about women, but what disturbed me is that the men started talking about how they should be kept in line. One of the guys began to narrate a story about how his wife had been acting up since she got a promotion at work and started earning more than him. He saw his wife's promotion and salary raise as a threat to his manhood. Bear in mind that his wife hadn't actually said anything or acted differently towards him after the promotion; he said he could just sense the disrespect and contempt and therefore felt the need to remind her who the man of the house is.

He went on to provoke her one day after work, and when she retaliated he slapped her right across the face and as she was about to open her mouth to say something another slap landed on her cheek, sending her right to the floor. He then went and sat in front of the TV and ordered her to dish up for him which she did without protest.

After hearing that story the most shocking thing for me was not the story itself, but rather the silence that followed. These guys are Christian men and you'd expect that one of them would say, "No, dude that's not right!" but no one said anything. Instead he was applauded.

This is what happens daily in our circles as men, not only with regard to domestic violence, but with other issues as well like taking care of the kids, infidelity and the like. Those who don't do these things keep quiet or lie just to fit in instead of calling such men out.

Normally we think that it is only women who are victims of toxic masculinity, but we men are too, and the examples provided in this book are proof of that. We act the way we do not because we are naturally abusers or undomesticated, but because of the societal norms created around masculinity. We forget that we have the opportunity to redefine what masculinity is.

Toxic masculinity is not a term used to describe certain men, but rather a certain behaviour pattern that all men are capable of adopting. When you read about sexual or domestic violence you almost immediately think about a creepy sinister character who's a low life, scum of the earth with no conscience or family — a man who lives in the shadows during the day and only emerges at night to pounce on innocent women. In actual fact it is men like you, my dear reader, men like me, men who are referred to as "real men". We are the perpetrators and perpetuators of toxic masculinity.

You might be thinking to yourself that you're not such a man because you've never laid a hand on a woman, but when you remain silent in situations like the one I mentioned above it means you are part of the problem. No one echoes it better than Jackson Katz on his TED talk when he says "Your silence is a form of consent and complicity."

Good men out there must take a stand and call out such behaviour so that those men who are perpetrators will lose their status among men. Such behaviour must be challenged because it is toxic to masculinity. However, these issues won't just evaporate by themselves, they need men who are willing to stand up for what is right and stop being bystanders. These issues, if ignored, will be the death of us because we'll have to lie or do things in secret because of the fear of being perceived as not being man enough. As men we should stop living by unrealistic masculine standards that are not attuned to the realities of modern life.

This narrow definition of masculinity is what leads most men to drug addiction and suicide. Men are said to be strong and don't show any sign of weakness, so when life gets to us we feel forced to suppress our feelings and pretend that we are fine when we are not. This narrow definition of masculinity does us more harm than good.

SEX

YOU CANNOT WRITE A BOOK for men and not have a chapter about sex — never! The problem, though, is that we men apply the Golden Rule in our approach to sex: Do unto others as you would have them do unto you. No! *Ayidumi kanjalo uma izosuka.* What sex means to men is different to what it means to women, and the sooner we understand that the healthier our sex life will be.

When we have conversations about sex with other men they turn into narcissist discussions about us men and what we want. We understand sex to be about us men only — this is what I learned in the streets. We are taught that it is men who need sex and for women it's a want, a desire they can live without. Whenever we have sex it is done to satisfy the man's craving and thewoman is there to assist us in achieving that. Women end up not being interested in it not because they don't love sex as much we do, but because our approach to sex is from a male's perspective.

Men need sex to enable them to love and be intimate. A man is a different being after sex — he's loving, open and will share even the darkest secrets in his heart; women love that man. When I'm stressed or can't sleep I don't need to discuss anything with anyone, I just need sex to reboot. Yet for my wife it's not like that; she needs love to have sex. Let's use the same scenario: When my wife is stressed out any sexual advances repulse her. She wants to talk and vent and only then can we have sex — once she feels the love and attention from her man. If we married men want to have a great sex life we need to change our patriarchal approach to sex.

As Mark Gungor puts it, "When you have one member in the relationship who needs love, closeness and intimacy *before* wanting sex, and another member in a relationship who can't really feel love, closeness, and intimacy until *after* sex, you have a problem. One can't help but wonder if the whole sex thing isn't some kind of cosmic joke. Yet, what if God designed this to be so on purpose? What if instead of arguing with each other and judging each other as perverts or frigid prudes, we worked at understanding and accommodating each other? This would mean we would have to treat sex as a way to serve the one we love.

"When sex is viewed as a way to love and serve each other in marriage, it brings a whole new order to human sexuality. Imagine a husband who cares enough to remember to practice those typical after-sex soft, caring feelings *before* sex in order to trigger sexual desire in his wife."

Change your usual approach to the one that stimulates her sexual desires and see how things change. The first and most important thing to note in the above passage is to view sex as another way of loving and serving each other. It then stops being about the man's self-gratification and is about the woman as well. Once you understand this as a man you'll learn to delay the urge to cum until she gets an orgasm. Please read that sentence again.

This is where you learn that the stuff you see in the movies is not true. In sex scenes in the movies lovers always reach a climax at the same time. Always. However that seldom occurs in real life. The first round normally belongs to the man and the second one, if you get to it, belongs to her. But to be on the safe side one should capitalize on the first round and serve her by delaying your climax because in most marriages a second round is as unlikely as lighting striking the same spot twice.

The second thing you must take from the passage above is viewing sex as a process for her that begins outside the walls of your bedroom. You must learn to prepare her during the day or on your way home — you know, like the old cars that needed to idle and warm up first before you could drive off to work. Experts say cars built before the '80s used oil as thick as molasses, and for the oil to do its job of lubricating the important parts in the engine it needed some warming up. Think of your woman like that too — for her to enjoy sex you need to warm her up. A text message to your wife that says "I miss my beautiful and sexy wife" can be a start when you want some. For us men, just seeing her thighs can be enough to take us from zero to a hundred, but for her it's different.

DIMINISHING SEX LIFE

'M SURE WE'VE ALL SEEN a movie or read a magazine where a spouse complains about how seldom they have sex in their marriage. And we all think to ourselves that when we get married we won't be that boring — we'll have sex at least twice a day seven days a week. How naïve!

While talking to a group of married men recently this is what dawned on me: Sex while living together and sex when staying apart is different. When you're living apart you don't get to see each other every day and therefore it becomes a luxury, a rare commodity. When you see her you become a cave man and you go for more than two rounds a day because you treat each day of sex as if it's your last. However, when you live together it's a different story because you know that she's still going to be there tomorrow, the day after tomorrow and for the rest of your life basically.

"Pssh!" some of you might exclaim, but the truth is, the sex life diminishes either way. For some it's due to the lifestyle they lead, and for others it's because their plates become too full as they try to build a future for their family. The point is, it will diminish. Before marriage, when you don't live together, it becomes the only thing you want to do when you meet. However, when you live together it becomes the last thing you do because you both know that even the bed that you're doing it on had to be bought at some stage.

Before you were married other things in your lives didn't affect your sex life, but now too many things have to be in order for you two to enjoy it. It is almost impossible to have a great sex life when things are not good between you and your partner. Sex is no longer an isolated activity that is immune to other factors in your life; it now has to align with everything else you're juggling. It has to be in line with the bills, chores, state of your relationship, etc. For you to enjoy sex — or have it for that matter — the relationship has to be in a good state. If she comes home from work upset you have to allow her to vent and discuss the issue until she's calm, and that's when you can say, "Hey, I know something that can help you blow off some steam..."

A study printed in The University of Chicago Press about ten years ago stated that married couples are having sex about seven times a month, which is a little less than twice a week. In another study, it was reported that out of the 16 000 adults interviewed, the older participants were having sex about two to three times per month, while younger participants said they were having sex about once a week. In truth, a good sex life is relative; it varies from couple to couple. There is no one way of doing things — one couple can be happy doing it once a week, another two or maybe three times a week. The bottom line is that both parties should be happy with it. Compromise also plays a vital role in this.

While looking for inspiration for this book I was reading an article by Ayodeji Awosika on HuffPost. He says this about aspiring authors: "I get it ... some days you just don't *feel like writing*. The inspiration isn't there and you feel like you don't have anything important to say because you have so many other things to do — your job, your kids, your life, everything." After reading this I thought to myself, "For men this is how sex feels at times." Sometimes you just don't feel like doing it, and when you finally do your partner is not in the mood. This is where compromise comes in.

At times you won't feel like doing it for a numbers of reasons. It might be that you're watching a game of soccer and don't want to be disturbed or maybe you're just tired, but you may have to do it anyway just to make your partner happy — serve your woman, make her feel desirable by pleasing her in spite of your mood. To a man, when a woman says she's tired we take it as just that, she's tired. However, when a man says they are tired it communicates a lot of things to a woman, including the possibility that she's undesirable and not sexy.

Life gets to us and it's natural because as the years pass and you grow older, so do your relationships and the responsibilities that come with them. Usually during this stage where there's a diminishing sex life in the marriage men are tempted to go outside and try something new, confusing taste with excitement. They think a new cookie tastes better than their wife's when in reality that is not the case. New cookies are not better than your partner's, it is just the excitement, the thrill of something new, something forbidden that fools men into infidelity.

After a while, when the excitement wanes, these men just move onto yet another tastier cookie and the cycle continues until they wear themselves out or put everyone they are involved with at risk due to their unhealthy sex lives. The diminishing sex life shouldn't be perceived as a lack of passion and desire; instead see it as an opportunity for you and your wife to service and love one another with every opportunity you get.

INFIDELITY

THIS IS A VERY CHALLENGING chapter to write for people are very sensitive and defensive about it, but I had to write it. Those who do it have apparently "legit" reasons why they are doing it so that they can sleep better at night, and those who aren't doing it are very judgmental and don't understand why one would do such a thing. I'll try to deal with it as impartially as I can, but still honestly and not shy away from the truth.

The truth is, after being married for a while you'll probably get more attention from outside than you do in your relationship. Marriage is like most things in life; when you've desired something for a while and finally acquire it at first you can't get your hands or mind off it — until you get used to it, and then you start paying less attention to it.

Think of your first car — after you bought it you probably washed it every other day and didn't want people to eat or smoke in it. I had a colleague who even went as far as sleeping in his car the day he bought it. However, a year down the line you'd go a week without washing it and when you do it's out of necessity not love. That relationship with inanimate objects is no different when it comes to our partners in relationships. Soon we reach that stage after the honeymoon phase. That is completely normal; it happens in all relationships. Our wives can't be expected to be constantly stroking our egos around the clock when they have careers and other responsibilities that need their attention.

In his book *Understanding the Purpose of Men*, Myles Munroe refers to ego as a sexual trap. He writes that "Affairs develop because men want to prove they are still attractive to women. The thrill comes from knowing that someone still finds them romantically appealing. It feels good to a man to know that a woman thinks he's intelligent or handsome, that she enjoys talking with him, that she likes the way he thinks, that she finds him exciting to be with." No matter how many compliments a wife gives to her man, the very same compliment coming from a different woman somehow sounds different and has a feel-good factor to it because it comes from an unexpected source.

The impact of an act is amplified when it comes from a person you're not expecting it from. For example, if your enemy bad mouthed you it wouldn't bother you because you expect such actions from an enemy, but should your best friend or partner do the very same thing you'd be gutted because you don't expect pain from a loving place. Most women know how to use this to their advantage and most men still fall for it.

This is a man's problem, though, not a woman's.

I've heard countless pastors and relationship experts talk about how a woman should spice things up in the bedroom to keep her man from cheating, saying if she does this and that her man won't find a reason to go out and find comfort in another woman's arms. Ironically, though, when I talk to friends and colleagues who do cheat on their wives, the reasons they give 90% of the time, if not 100%, is not because of what is lacking at home or what their wives are unable to provide, it is just for their own selfish reasons. There's nothing a wife can do to stop a man from cheating if he is not willing to stop himself from doing it.

Bear in mind that there's no such thing as a perfect partner. There's no woman who'll be everything you need in life, but the media will continuously tell us that if she's really the one she'll tick all the boxes and you'll get 100% of what you want in a relationship or marriage. What a fallacy! The current generation would probably call it BS. In reality you are most likely to get 80% of the 100% you want in a relationship. (Please give me some credit, I didn't learn about this from a Tyler Perry movie.)

Ever heard of the 80/20 rule? For those who don't know it, the 80/20 rule is basically the theory that says, in a healthy relationship you only get 80% of what you want in a relationship, but it's okay because the 80% you *do* get should be sufficient. For example, I love soccer and follow the best competitive leagues in the world, but my wife doesn't; she's tried to follow the sport just to make me happy but it's just not in her. As much as it would be amazing if my wife was as interested in the sport as I am, I can live with the fact that she isn't and I'm happy that she allows me to take control of the remote almost every day of the week to watch it.

I know there are other things that she would love for me to be or be interested in. For example whenever we watch reality shows with husbands who are passionate about cooking and are really good at it, I'd see in her eyes that she wishes she had a husband like that, but unfortunately her husband can't cook to save his life. The point is none of us is perfect, hence you'll get the 80% in a relationship and get glimpses of the 20% from other people, but that shouldn't be interpreted as there being something missing from your life.

Some people expect their partners to be perfect and know everything that will satisfy their needs. When a man meets a female colleague who shares the same passion as him for sports, for example, he suddenly thinks there's something lacking in his marriage because his wife can't meet those needs. Men like that often end up going for that 20% only to realize later that what they lost was worth more than what they currently have.

One thing you must know for sure when it comes to this subject is that it has nothing to do with your partner; it's a decision that's deeply personal. Have you ever been told that once you find the right woman you'll stop cheating? That's a lie. If a man's faithfulness isdependent on his partner's treatment of him, well I can tell you now that it is only a matter of time before he starts seeing other women. Do you think that man is going to remain faithful when there's constant fighting that lasts several days? Or when his partner doesn't trust him even though he knows that he's been faithful to her? No, he won't, because he's only being faithful for her, not himself.

Remember when I spoke earlier in the book about that picture you should envision of yourself? Being faithful to your partner should be in that vision as well. For one to remain faithful it has to be primarily about yourself and your deeply held beliefs or principles — your personal ethics, not worldly ones.

In my case, for example, I choose to remain faithful to my wife not out of the fear of going to hell in the afterlife, but because cheating is one of the leading causes of divorce in today's society. Should I start with even one incident I would probably open the door for many more and might end up losing Thuli which is a reality I can't even begin to imagine, and even if I can imagine it I don't want to experience it.

I also love tranquillity and coming home to a peaceful environment. Should I cheat on my wife I would not only hurt her, but would also bring pain and chaos into my world. Only a foolish person would want to invite that kind of pain into their own life. When an environment is chaotic like that it's almost impossible to be focused and productive in other spheres of your life. For you to be productive in other sphere of your life you need to curb that part of your temperament and resist the temptation to cheat.

Look at it this way — the one thing that makes us different from animals is our intelligence; should that be taken away from us humanity as we know it would cease to exist because there wouldn't be any difference between us and all the other animals. My point is that we are not an instinctive species; almost everything we do is done consciously. In order for our intelligence to bear fruit and for our purpose in life to be realized there should be a higher level of focus on that aspect of our life.

Let me be practical. Sex with your wife probably occupies 20% percent of your life and the other 80% is for school, work, spirituality and the like. Now if you add another sexual partner into your life they'd eat into that 80%, and before you know it, several sexual partners later, more than 50% of your life is driven by hormones (your intelligence commandeered by them) and the meaningfulness and joy that one gets from living out their purpose or building a successful functional family unit is no longer there. All you're left with is a gaping hole in its place because half of your time and money was spent pleasing other women and poorly investing in a life of promiscuity.

Those are some of my reasons for remaining faithful. I know that human beings are innately selfish, and when push comes to shove we are most likely to go with the option that benefits us, so if you want to be faithful to your partner you should have reasons that are of benefit to you — reasons why being loyal benefits you and your wellbeing. Doing it for your wife because you love her and don't want to hurt her is a by-product of that. You'll never consistently, over a long period of time, do something that doesn't benefit you; that egotistical intrinsic part of you as a man won't allow it.

WHITE ELEPHANT IN THE ROOM

IT IS ONE OF THE most frowned upon things and one that men don't like talking about but still continue to do even after they get married. Brace yourself and take a deep breath: masturbation! I've yet to meet a man who doesn't do it. They won't admit it, but most men do it. One of the things that men I've had discussions with like about masturbation is that one gets the pleasure without putting in too much effort or going through the foreplay.

Here's a good analogy describing the two processes in an article by Cosmo Frank which appeared in *Cosmopolitan* magazine: "Sometimes when you're hungry, you just want a good steak. You go to the market, you get a good cut of meat, you make your own marinade and tenderize the meat. You put it on the grill and make some potatoes in the oven. It's a process, but it's worth it for the end result. Other times, you say 'Screw it' and eat a couple fistfuls of dry cereal while you lie on the couch in sweatpants. They both satisfy your hunger and the result is the same: You ate. Just like sex and masturbation, the result is the same: you cum. However, just like no one is going to tell you dry cereal is better than steak, masturbation isn't really better than sex. I can assure you that no man thinks that."

If you still masturbate when you're married or in a long-term relationship just know that you are not alone, as the above excerpt suggests. Feel guilty after doing it? Feel worse than crap or useless? The answer is still the same: most men do anyway. For some this is due to the religion they subscribe to or how it is perceived in the society they grew up in. Whatever the reason may be, men continue to overwork their right hand (or left hand if they're left handed).

To make you feel better about yourself, Dr Michael Ashworth writes that research shows that those people who masturbate more also have more (and more satisfying) sex. That's probably because a person who masturbates continues to be in touch with their own body and their own sexual needs and desires more than someone who doesn't. It also means they are getting their sexual needs met as often as they'd like, putting less pressure on their partner to fulfil their sexual needs. You can take it as being an excuse by those who masturbate to make themselves feel better or as a reality that most men cannot escape, it's up to you.

For me personally, I feel that masturbation has a tendency to make men think that sex is only about them and their gratification. The material used while masturbating also makes men objectify women and pretty much expect them to fulfil fantasies that don't stem from love but lust. A man sees Pinky doing tricks on the internet and expects his wife to do the same — and enjoy it — forgetting that these are actors and will fake almost anything for the production to sell. This becomes a problem, especially when unrealistic expectations are reinforced by the material used to masturbate. When his partner can't meet those expectations the man often feels justified in going outside his marriage to find a person who will.

We forget that we men are not as perfect as we think we are when it comes to sex, and because our women don't want to bruise our fragile egos they keep quiet and are patient with our mediocre performances. If you want to try something new because you genuinely want to spice up your sex life that'sfine, but don't expect your woman to be an expert in every position out there.

I've had conversations with several men who talk about how sex workers give good fellatio but when they get home it's just not the same. In my head, I'm thinking, "How do you expect a girl who you probably met at church and who has one or two exes (because when they have more exes than that they are deemed unworthy as marriage material by our standards) to be as good as someone who's been doing it every day for years with different men?"

If we're realistic and have enough patience to teach and also learn from our women, we'll reach amazing heights in unison. However, as long as we continue to interpret what we see on porn websites as reality, then our chances of attaining a great sexual experience are no better than a mad man's hopes of reaching a rainbow.

TOUCHY SUBJECTS

QUALITY TIME

MOST men struggle with this concept. Sex is what comes to our minds when we hear the words "quality time", but what women mean by this is what Gary Chapman describes as giving someone your undivided attention. That does not include sitting on the couch watching television together because that way it's the TV not your spouse that has your attention. Quality time means sitting on couch with the TV off, looking at each other and talking.

Sadly, most of us men can't take our eyes off that enticing blue screen. Not because we don't enjoy talking to our partner, but because men in general don't like talking about their feelings. Quality time is something most men, including myself, struggle with because it requires us to open up and reveal our fears and insecurities. But at the end of the day it has to be done.

In our guy-circles we joke about it and say women are too demanding for asking that of us; how dare they? Friends aside, the reality is that you can't know your partner thoroughly if you don't have quality time. Lack of communication happens gradually, like soft drizzling rain; you take it for granted until eventually, if you stay in it long enough, you get thoroughly soaked.

Back in the day it was the TV or radio that posed a threat to quality time, but now it's our phones. The age of TV was better because you were able to leave it in your house when you went out, but we can't do that with our phones. They are with us everywhere we go, even in the toilet; the toilet used to be a sacred place and it allowed us time for some introspection (I'm dead serious right now) but not any more. In the township there used to be a saying that goes something like: No matter how much you try to escape your problems you'll come face to face with them when you are sitting alone on the toilet seat staring at that rusty door with yellow pages next to you. The mobile phone has taken that experience away from us!

It's a fact — phones make it harder to have quality time alone as a couple. But do not despair; quality time varies from couple to couple, and there is no one correct way of having it. Quality time discussions can happen on your way home after church or over dinner after work. The bottom line is there should be togetherness. As Tawny May puts it, "A central aspect of quality time is togetherness. And by togetherness I don't mean proximity. Togetherness has to do with focused attention." One can feel lonely with their partner right next to them when they're busy on their phone. Unfortunately I don't have any easy steps you can follow or five-ways-to-spend-quality-time-with-your-partner advice for you because each couple is different, but through communication with your partner you'll achieve that togetherness.

NOT EVERYONE IS MEANT TO BE IN A LONG-TERM RELATIONSHIP

I don't understand why most people think this statement only applies when you're referring to marriage and not to all relationships. Think about it: What is it about these people that they're not cut out for marriage? My guess is probably the same reasons they are not cut out for a long-term relationship. And there's nothing wrong with that. Once again society has erred in thinking that we are all the same.

In an article shared on *RelRule.com* I read that,"While modern media keeps on shoving the idea of lifelong romances down peoples' throats, it's very easy for people to forget that there are other options. If you feel like you're not really built for a long-term romance, then that's okay. You should embrace that part of yourself. Besides, the only logical reason as to why you would want to be in a long-term relationship in the first place would be because you genuinely want to; it can't be because that's what you think society expects of you."

Being in a monogamous relationship is a choice and a full time job with no vacation. You don't take a break from it and decide to see other people; there is no age limit to it. You can get married in your 20s, 30s or 40s and that's fine, but setting the same timeline for everyone may be the root to most of the problems we have today.

EXES

I grew up in a staunch Christian family where *umjolo* is a sin. However, the older I got, the more I realized how misinformed my parents were in assuming that a marriage is only a spiritual thing that doesn't need experience or coaching. The more relationships one has, the more knowledgeable one becomes of oneself.

Most men underestimate the role of an ex in their lives because they are usually a reminder of the past, their failures and past selves. What they fail to see is that your ex prepares you for your future wife. Here's a simple analogy: Think of your ex as an internship that teaches you everything you need to know about your dream job, and think of your future wife as the actual job. Mistakes and slip ups are easily forgiven during an internship, but not so much in the actual job. An ex allows you to know more about yourself when it comes to relationships. You get to know what annoys you and what makes you happy. Maybe in your teenage years you thought you were into tall, slim women, but when you finally dated one you realized that actually you don't really care about a woman's body shape, size or looks as long as she's humble and ambitious; you learn that what matters to you is her character.

Apart from learning about the kind of woman you want, you also learn about your own strengths and weaknesses. As stated in one of *eHarmony's* articles, "Think back to the arguments you used to have with your ex. What did they throw back at you? Was it that you were too picky? Too passive? Too grumpy? Whatever it was, the chances are that they had a point. Of course insults that are spoken purely in anger don't count, but consider the other stuff said when you were disagreeing. Think your ex might have had a point? Good. You now get to go forward with full knowledge of your flaws and become an even better partner in your next relationship."

This is important because a relationship is not only about the other person, but you as well. One of the mistakes we make in relationships is to be quick to point out the other person's flaws and forget that we are not perfect either. The sad thing is that most of us refuse to acknowledge that part because it will force us to confront those things that we hate the most about ourselves — our weaknesses. It is evident that all prior relationships are a learning curve and prepare us for the one we will spend the rest of our lives in.

Before getting married a man needs to experience heartaches, disappointment, crying over someone and being cheated on by their partner (although perhaps that is pushing it a little bit too far). All those experiences help give one a reality check when it comes to relationships and idealized standards.

FINANCES

Make sure you have a steady source of income before you even think of proposing. The line "As long as we have each other nothing else matters" doesn't work in real life; once the honeymoon phase wanes there will be scrutiny as to what each person has brought to the table. Having said that, though, your roles in the relationship shouldn't be defined by material things or what each person has. With the high rate of unemployment in South Africa there's no guarantee that tomorrow you'll still be in the job that you currently have, and although that will bring financial strain it's important that it doesn't affect your marriage and who you are.

In today's society a man is no longer a man if he can't provide for his family, but somehow a woman is not considered less of a woman when there's an aunty or helper in the house doing all the cooking, cleaning and all the other stuff that traditionally defines women. Why is that? It's because your self-worth or identity is not defined by the title you hold at work or the money you bring into the relationship. Once our identity is linked to societal roles instead of purpose it will create problems in our marriages.

For example, a man who needs a leadership position to feel worthy won't be at ease in the same way as a man who sees himself as a leader even if he has no position at all. Look at a man like Nelson Mandela, for example, who was an attorney and chairman of Umkhonto we Sizwe (MK) before being imprisoned. His incarceration on Robben Island meant he was stripped of those titles, but because his identity was not linked to tangible things, prison couldn't contain him and the conditions there didn't dampen his leadership.

Basically the point is this: even if the woman brings all the money into the house your manhood should still be intact because your identity is not linked to your employment status. However, to ensure the man does not feel emasculated if his wife is the only one working, money must not be mistaken for power or be used as a weapon to control one's partner. As a man, when you are employed or earn more than your woman make sure that you treat her the same way as you would want her to treat you if the tables were turned. If there was only an "I" in your salary, don't expect a "we" in hers.

When things got serious between Thuli and I, after I paid the first instalment of the lobolo, I voluntarily showed her my pay slip so that she knew how much I earned. I did that because it would enable her to make sound financial decisions in the house, and to make her feel like the money I earn is *our* money. I was the only one working at the time, so I had to lead by example so that when she got employed she would know that her money is our money too. Had I decided to hide my payslip in order to gain power through decision making in the house, what would stop her from doing the same once she started working? It would be even worse if I lost my job and she became the bread winner, because with the tables turned I would feel emasculated if she decided for both of us how her money should be spent. As it turned out, three years after we got married I lost my job, and guess what happened … her money was our money and all the bank cards remained with me; it was as if nothing had changed.

CURFEW

We all have a curfew, and the key to your wife's happiness depends on it. Most men deny this and say they can go home whenever they want to, but when we are hanging out and it starts to get dark you'll hear stuff like "I forgot something at home" or "Something just came up and I've got to run". The truth of the matter is that all married men have a curfew. This curfew won't be directly communicated to you, though, instead it will develop right at the back of your head — that little voice in your mind yelling at you while you're hanging out with your friends is not your conscience, it's your wife. If she does set a curfew, try to respect it and don't trivialize it because it doesn't make sense to you. Part of being married means respecting your partner's wishes, even if they may not be as important in your eyes. There will be things that you'll ask of your wife which won't mean as much to her as they do to you, but you'll also want her to respect them to make you happy.

HABITS

Marriage has a lot to do with compromise, and that word is at times thought of as a magic wand that can erase just about every habit you don't like about your partner. Please understand that I'm not talking about toxic habits like drinking one's salary away in a weekend. In marriage minor things tend to be put under a magnifying glass and some things may really upset your partner in ways you can't imagine. Small things such as drinking milk from the carton or not putting the glass back where you found it can cause you to sleep with your backs turned against each other at night. With that being said, one must accept that some habits won't go away no matter how much you fight them.

I come from a family that's been digging for gold in their noses for centuries; it's a habit I don't like myself but I just can't help it when I'm at home. It's like a disease, and if there was a rehab centre for nose pickers I'd be the first one in the queue. My poor wife has done everything in her power to get me to stop but has failed. She also has her own habits that rub me the wrong way; some she has ceased and others I have to tolerate. That's marriage for you — accept that certain habits took vows with you on the day of your wedding when you said "till death do us part". Such habits shouldn't be interpreted as a sign of disrespect.

15

WHAT MEN WANT

I'M NOT AN ADVOCATE FOR men and am not even an admin of a men's group on WhatsApp. However, in my research this is what I found to be the oxygen for men — literally the thing that most men need to survive in a relationship. I use the word oxygen seriously, because that's how much men need respect in a relationship.

In his book *Laugh Your Way to a Better Marriage*, Mark Gungor writes that respect means that a man wants to be "held in esteem and to be shown consideration and appreciation — even when he makes mistakes. He wants to be a hero, especially in the eyes of his bride. What I'm saying is that men need to be respected for who they are, not for what they do. If they don't feel respected, they can't survive. It gets harder and harder for them to breathe (emotionally)."

I know the last part sounds sexist, but that's a topic for another day. The bottom line is that men inherently feel the need to be respected — unconditionally. Not the type of respect that is given when we do well and is taken away when we slip up, or the kind given when we get a high paying job and taken away when we're retrenched.

Let me use a familiar scenario that I often witness in South Africa. Unemployment is high, not only for new graduates or youth, but for the veterans as well; I'm seeing more and more fathers and husbands losing their jobs. When this happens most men feel emasculated. People think the inability to provide financially is what emasculates a man, but that's not it. A man can be unemployed but still be just as ambitious and optimistic as he was before — still feel like he can conquer the world in spite of his predicament. However, a home that is devoid of respect and admiration smothers his ability to see past his current situation, rendering him useless.

Unemployment is temporary, but disrespect can be permanent. Men are generally insecure and that's why a woman is referred to as a man's pillar. Now imagine what happens to a temple, no matter how big it may be, when its pillar collapses. Complete annihilation occurs. The man becomes like a dog with its tail between its legs and there's nothing pretty about that picture. A dog like that will end up being despised by its very master. In the same way, women will tell you that there's nothing as unattractive as a man who lacks ambition.

Another contributing factor in the world today that leads to a lack of respect is that smart and successful women think they don't need men. Don't get me wrong, not being reliant on men is great and should be applauded, and that will inspire a new generation of women who know that they don't need a man to survive or to be successful in life. However, it becomes a problem when a man is made to feel that he's not needed in a relationship.

Are most men intimidated by independent women? Probably. Are they intimidated by her achievements or the fear of not being treated like a man? I think it's the latter in most cases. Dating expert Joshua Pompey once said: "Obviously there will always be men, regardless of how much the times change, who hold up the male chauvinism glory days of the 1950s as the golden social model. With that said, for the most part, men are not intimidated by strong and successful women. In fact, most men find these qualities very attractive and will brag to their friends and family about what a smart, great girl they have found."

In today's society we should expect that more and more households will have women earning more than their men, and that shouldn't be a problem. The problem starts when money or a job title is used to determine the treatment one should get or the level of respect one deserves — when value is put on a career and material possessions rather than a person's character. What such women fail to understand is that what matters at the end of the day is the warmth we bring to our homes and the way we make each other feel. What you are outside the confines of your home or what you bring to the table matters not to most men.

CONCLUSION

NOTHING IS AS HARD AS finding yourself and what you're meant to be in this life. However, once you do find your purpose, you start living life in an effective manner. You focus on things that hone your skills and enhance you as an individual; you simply focus on the important things. The same is true of marriage; when you've got a clear vision of the kind of husband you want to be and the legacy you want to leave behind you'll start focusing on things that help you achieve those goals. That vision will help you navigate the world and pull out the weeds that are a hindrance in your life. The vision will channel your focus onto the things that will help you achieve those goals; it will attract people who share the same sentiments as you about marriage and allow for positive dialogues and stories that resonate with you and your goals instead of negative ones.

Remember that what you feed your mind affects your behaviour and perception of the world. If the people you've surrounded yourself with — both online and in real life — only have negative things to say about marriage and women you'll unconsciously internalize that and make it your lived experience. Notice how unsafe we feel in our own homes because of the crime stories we see on TV; even if we've never had any such incidents in our own neighbourhood, because we've seen it on TV we make it our reality. What you feed your mind and the people you surround yourself with are key to becoming a good husband.

That's the first thing to be aware of. Secondly, be patient with your wife; you have a whole lifetime to get to know each other. Don't expect her to treat you the same way your mom treated your dad from the outset. By the time I reached maturity my parents had already been together for more than 20 years. I only really started assessing their marriage from its twentieth year onwards and used that as a standard to judge my own marriage in its first year. I used my mom who'd been in it for 20 years to judge my wife after only one year of marriage. Now that's a bit unfair, yet that's what most people are doing. I wasn't there in my parents' first ten years of marriage when the two personalities were constantly clashing with each other, I only got to experience it after those constantly clashing personalities merged into one.

Don't rush it; don't be too hasty to reach that level because you'll cause your own demise. Enjoy the process, learn to love and forgive even when you don't feel like forgiving because forgiveness is a choice, not a feeling. Learn not to hold grudges by focusing on the present and not the past. This journey is beautiful. I look at my life in my twenties and the memories that Thuli and I share and I wouldn't have it any other way. Having a person next to you who experiences life with you is almost like having a video recording of your childhood; when you watch it as an adult you realize that what makes these memories so dear and priceless is not that it's you in the video, but that there's another person who was holding the camera and experiencing those life moments with you. When you were down and out, when things weren't going your way and equally when you were on top of the world she was there with you every step of the way. Tell me, my dear reader, how can I not count myself lucky?

To make it simple, if you want a successful marriage love your wife wholeheartedly and commit to working on your marriage, not being distracted by everything that's going on around you. Have a vision of what you want your marriage to be and what your role is in that marriage, and make sure you're both on the same page. Marriage can be a wonderful adventure if you and your partner are working together in the same direction.

www.ingramcontent.com/pod-product-compliance
Lightning Source LLC
Chambersburg PA
CBHW061334040426
42444CB00011B/2911